Shirley Pickard

Angels are Everywhere

Fictional / Nonfiction
Inspirational Poetry
And Food for Thought
Verses from King James Version
Graphics and illustrations used by Dover Publications, Inc., with permission from Minneola, New York. Painting was by the author.

Note for Librarians: A cataloguing record for this book is available from Library and Archives Canada at www.collectionscanada.ca/amicus/index-e.html
ISBN 1-4251-0922-5

Trafford's print shop runs on "green energy" from solar, wind and other environmentally-friendly power sources.

TRAFFORD PUBLISHING™
Offices in Canada, USA, Ireland and UK

Book sales for North America and international:
Trafford Publishing, 6E–2333 Government St.,
Victoria, BC V8T 4P4 CANADA
phone 250 383 6864 (toll-free 1 888 232 4444)
fax 250 383 6804; email to orders@trafford.com
Book sales in Europe:
Trafford Publishing (UK) Limited, 9 Park End Street, 2nd Floor
Oxford, UK OX1 1HH UNITED KINGDOM
phone +44 (0)1865 722 113 (local rate 0845 230 9601)
facsimile +44 (0)1865 722 868; info.uk@trafford.com
Order online at:
trafford.com/06-2680

10 9 8 7 6 5 4 3 2 1

Dedication

This book is dedicated to my late father, Howard Stanfield, *1898–March 20, 1994*, and my wonderful mother, Dorothy Stanfield, who is age 91. It's also dedicated to my family and friends. All those who believed in me and supported me with prayers and words of encouragement.

This book is also dedicated to my sister-in-law, Betty Pickard, and my brother-in-law, Larry Pickard, who has always been there for me.

Note of Thanks

First of all, I give thanks to God for this book. I pray that someone can read this book and get to know Jesus as their savior.

Many special thanks to my children, to my friends in Reidsville and Eden, North Carolina, to my friends in New York and Pelham, North Carolina and to my entire church family

Introduction:

Inspirational Poetry

Soul winning poetry by Shirley S. Pickard.

God cares; He wants everyone to be with Him in heaven, so He sent His son, Jesus to be your Savior and your best friend. We communicate with God through Jesus Christ. He also sent His "Holy spirit" to comfort us and His angels to deliver a message.

Ordinary people are angels too, so open the door to your heart and let God in, and you'll find that at the lowest point in your life ordinary angels will knock on your door, or call you on the phone with a message that you really needed to hear. Listen to their message. My soul cries out—I won't complain, because I have a special friend name Jesus. He is my rock.

A conversation with God is soothing to the soul. Just call Him up—He'll give you joy untold. Sow seeds of kindness, always smile, and fly away with Jesus. Angels are everywhere. You never know when you're entertaining a child of the king.

Lift up your hands in the sanctuary, and bless the Lord. Psalm 134:2.

On The Wings of An Angel

While driving down the road one day, a car came speeding straight my way. With fear in my heart as death drew near, thank You God for keeping me here.

Somehow the car was no longer there. A stranger came out of nowhere. The enemy thought he had me. I was riding on the wings of an angel

On the wings of an angel is how we survive each day. Bad things could have happened. God took them away on—on the wings of an angel.

On the wings of an angel, God stands afloat. Close your eyes and whisper a prayer. Remember God's angels are everywhere.

They watch over us as we sleep each night, awaken us each morning to see the bright sunlight. He gives us fresh air to breathe, and beautiful things to see. Thank You God for loving me.

Guardian Angels

An angel appeared before me in the form of a light. I stopped to stare at it with all my might. As strange as it may seem, I was not afraid, as that light bounced around my head. There it was a message it was trying to convey, thou it was silent, not a word came my way. It must be my guardian angel. I thought because I felt so safe and protected, when ever your angels come around you'll feel connected. Protected from crime protected from crooks. They all have names written in the book. Some angels are invisible to the eye, we can't see them as they float around the sky. Angels can be good or bad, they protected me from that accident I should have had. They protected me as I slept. Many nights unknown, things they do for us, only God knows. I thank God for angels every night. I thank God for sending me guardian angels to make everything alright.

Angels Are Ordinary People

God loves ordinary people like you and I, not so high and mighty to reach for the sky. Stretch forth your hands and he'll reach down His hands for you. He's never too busy to see us through.

Angels are ordinary people sent by God to do His will, He uses our hands. He uses our feet. There's angelic powers, wherever we meet.

Ordinary people are not so small. God uses those who don't stand tall. Ordinary people become extraordinary helpers for the kingdom of God. Angels walk the earth each and every day. They're here to help us along the way.

I'm Just Asleep

I'm not deceased, I'm just asleep, my soul doesn't rest in peace. Oh, sweet sleep, oh sweet sleep. Just like the rising sun. Don't weep for me my child, for my life has just begun.

I'm in His arms, and I'm so glad no greater love no one has ever had. Just close your eyes, and say "good night". God will lead you to the light.

Hello mother, hello father, there's my brother too. He didn't let us sleep too late. We all made it through. You know, I was just asleep, but now I'm heaven bound. The angels came and took me, when there was no one else around.

A Place Called Heaven

We'll go sailing through the air, to a beautiful city where the streets are paved in gold, "a place called heaven". Don't you want to go?

Children are playing and singing in perfect harmony; oh how beautiful is that city, "a place called heaven". It's an open door. We claim it by faith, we live by His grace. Accept Jesus as your Lord. Don't you want to go?

With wide-open arms, Jesus will meet you there. With a chant and a smile, He'll say "come here my child." I've been waiting for you. Let me wipe away your tears. I'll take away your pain. This is "a place called heaven", where you have nothing to lose but all to gain. Don't you want to go?

The Holy Spirit

Just like the mighty wind that blows, we don't know from whence it came or where it goes. The comforter comes and takes control, don't quench it. It is the Holy Ghost.

It gets all in your hands, it gets all in your feet, when your body starts to move, you never miss a beat. If you don't know God, I suggest you give Him a try. He's that Holy Spirit sent to you from on high.

He'll never leave you nor forsake you, the best friend that I know. When you think that it's all over. He sends a comforter - the Holy Ghost.

The Holy Spirit will take you places where you've never been. Then He will bring you back to reality again. He's a perfect gentleman; oh I love Him so. Tarry until you find Him. He'll never let you go.

Open The Door

God stands at the door of your heart each and everyday. If you open your heart, he'll come in to stay. He came into my heart one day. Every since then, I've felt okay.

He walks with me, He talks with me. Lets me know how special I am. When you open that door you'll find He's always around. He'll pick you up, clean you up, and plant your feet on higher ground.

Knock—knock, who's there? God is there. Open the door and let Him in. He'll fill your heart with untold joy, place a smile on your face and save your soul.

I Won't Complain

I won't complain; I'll just do the best I can. Oh, how my soul long for a breath of fresh air; your breath is so sweet as it sweeps across my face and through my hair.

When I see the beautiful flowers that bloom and gaze up to the beautiful blue skies, I realize that no one can give such a beautiful gift as this. Thank you dear Lord, "I won't complain".

If you feel like complaining, "Just call Him up". Tell Jesus all about it. He'll whisper back to you, "Do the best you can and I'll do the rest". Reach up your hands to me, and I'll catch you. Together we'll walk hand in hand to that mansion in the sky. "Just call Him up", don't complain.

When life's problems seem to get you down—God cares.

When friends are a few, there's no one around—God cares.

He cares, when we're right. He cares, when we're wrong. God's love is forever present to keep us strong.

His love for us is higher than the highest mountain, and deeper than the deepest sea. The precious blood He shed was just for you and me.

God cares about your problems. God cares about your needs. He wants to hear your story. He promises to supply all our needs according to His riches in glory.

A Conversation With God

Good morning God; thank you for watching over me last night as I slept. You woke me up and I still have breath, "thank you".

God, there's so much I want to tell you. I don't know where to begin. You've given me a brand new day. I saw the sun rise, and I can hear the birds singing again.

God, before I begin this day, I just want to stop and pray. I want you to know that I love you so. Thank you for your grace and mercy that is brand new everyday. Thank you for walking ahead of me to make a way.

Thank you! God for whispering in my ear, when no-one else wanted to hear. A conversation with God is like a peace of gold. A conversation with God will never be told.

A Special Friend

I met a special friend many years ago. He is very special. How I love Him so. No matter what I'm going through, He's there until the end. He sticks closer than a brother. He's a special friend.

Each day new gifts I find. Not just a new day, but love, joy, and peace of mind. My secret desires, He knows them all. Whether they be great or small. Do you know Him? He loves you and me, a special friend is He.

Let me introduce you to Him today, He'll come into your heart to day. He's our Lord and Saviour, Jesus Christ. When all other friends turn their back, He's right there to hold your hand and lead you back on track.

The Blood

The blood that was shed over 2000 years ago has more power than man will ever know.

Jesus was the only one worthy to pay the price for His purpose here on earth was to save our life.

God loved us so much until he gave His only son. No good deeds or no good works could ever to Him repay.

It's through God's grace and mercy that we'll some day see His face. There's a cross we all must bear.

Jesus has already paid the price trust in Him to save your life. All power is in the blood. God sent his only so from above.

No greater love—we shall not stray, draw near to Him and He'll draw near to you. Never forget to pray. The blood will never loose its power. "The blood".

No Cross—no Crown

At the end of each storm is sunshine.
At the end of each cloud a rainbow.
At the end of each valley a hilltop.
At the end of pain, there's relief.
At the end of sorrow, there's joy.
But remember there's got to be pain in your life to appreciate the sunshine.
No cross—no crown.

God Wants Us To Have More

God wants us to have more, if we give more, we'll have more. Give more tithing of the first fruit.

More love, more joy, more peace, more giving, and less taking. Give more faith, more wisdom, and grace.

More praying, reading and declaring God's Word. Seek first the kingdom of God and all good things shall be added.

Forgive others and bring your offerings unto God for His word is true. We must forgive others as He forgives you. Your offerings will be accepted and blessing will fall through.

The more you give, the more He'll give to you. Just keep giving and forgiving. The more He'll give to you.

Sow a Seed

Sow a seed of kindness. Sow a seed of love. All good seeds are sent from heaven above.

Sow a seed of sharing. Sow a seed of time. Sow a seed of friendship and friendship is what you'll find.

Sow a seed to the needy. Sow a seed to your neighbor. If you trust in God, He'll always show you favor.

Sow a seed of money. Sow a seed of prayer. Take your burdens to Jesus. He knows how much we can bear.

If you have a need, sow a seed and it will come right back to you.

If you sow a seed for Jesus, He'll always see you through.

Butterfly (I'll Fly Away)

God created creeping, crawling things, and many things that fly; however, there's none more beautiful than the butterfly.

They come in many color; purple, yellow, orange and red. No wonder we stop and stare as they fly around our head.

If I could have wings, the butterfly is what I'd be. When the storms of life are raging, I'll just fly away to be free.

Just like the butterfly. God wants us to fly away with Him. Fly through the winds, fly through the storms, there's a safety net in His arms.

Through the good and the bad, fly away with Jesus. I'll fly away. There's no other creation like me. I'll fly away. I'll be a butterfly. I'll fly away.

A Smile

What's in a smile that warms the heart? What's in a smile that seems to lighten the load of a busy day?

We may never know exactly what's in each smile. However, we all know that: A smile is a moment to cherish; a smile can be freely given; a smile can say "I like you" or "I love you".

What does it cost a man to smile? It costs him nothing. So, smile and the world will smiles with you.

When you are persecuted—smile.

When you are lied on and talked about—smile.

When your heart is breaking—smile.

When your world seems up side down—smile.

Just keep smiling, and the devil will wonder what you are smiling about. Selah

The Rainbow

God made a promise and we can't deny this earth shall not be destroyed by water but fire.

After the storms, strong wind and rain, just smell the freshness of the earth and its sweetness remains. Just look up and you'll see. Look to the east and to the west, you can't deny, for God put a rainbow in the sky.

The beautiful blue sky at the end of a storm. Sunshine awaits its turn to appear, while the shallow clouds in the western sky displays an array of many color. We cheer!

We can't see where it begins or where it ends, however, we can't deny that God put a rainbow in the sky. An awesome sight it is to see. He put it there for you and me.

Be Grateful

I was complaining about the rain, and then I saw a man that was blind. He couldn't see the beautiful sunshine, the snow, or the color of the sky.

He replied what a beautiful sound the rain makes as it falls on the ground. It makes the earth feel cool and smell so fresh.

Then I saw a beautiful pair of shoes that I just had to try them on, with anger in my heart as I placed them back. I can't wear these. They'll just hurt my feet.

Then I saw a man with no feet or legs. He was riding along in his wheel chair singing. He replied, "Just think how much money I save on shoes and socks, I will give these dollars to God".

Dear God, help us to be grateful for each day, for life, health, and strength, for eyes to see, for feet to walk, for food and shelter, most of all help us to be grateful for your Son, Jesus, who died for the redemption of our sins.

I Apologize

I apologize for all the times I should have kneeled to pray. Instead I went along trying to have things my way.

I apologize for not taking time to say thank you even when I knew that it was you who woke me up on time.

You gave me eyes to see and food to eat. Instead of giving you thanks I rolled over and went back to sleep.

Forgive me Lord for all that I should have done to glorify Jesus your one and only son. I apologize, Father for all that I've done wrong. I thought I was so strong.

Thank you for giving me another chance and the courage to admit I've been so wrong. Man kind looks on the outside but you can see deep within.

Whenever I fell short your grace and mercy drew me back again.

Thank you for saving me when I was deep in a world of sin with outstretched arms you welcomed me back and took me in.

I apologize for when I should have given to you my heart was filled with greed.

You taught me that in order to reap a harvest I must sow a seed. You taught me how to love, instead of hate, to pray and leave the pass behind. Only then shall we have joy, forgiveness, and peace of mind.

Father, thank you for forgiving me.

I apologize.

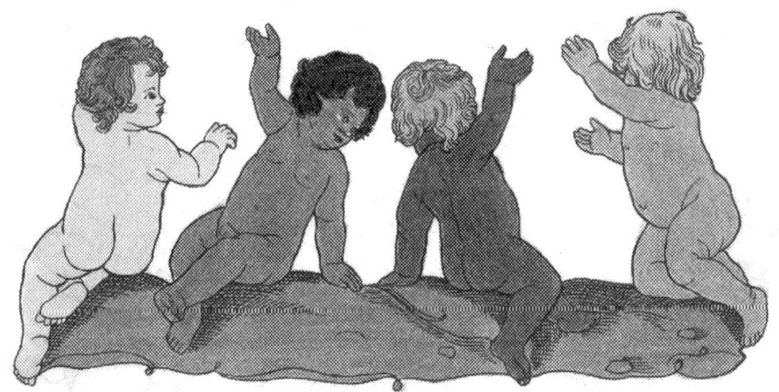

Giving Much, Expecting Nothing

Thank God for volunteers, giving of yourselves throughout the year, not waiting to be asked. Each performance is an unpaid task, and you go on giving cheerfully, So many places you could be, instead you're here with us, a helping hand that does not rush to do the things you've come to do.

There's so much that God has in store for you—telling jokes, playing games, real go getters, sharing joy, smiles, and love. To make others feel better—teaching, singing and covering with prayer, reminding little children that God really cares.

Diligently working as you go through life's trials, willing to go that extra mile. I see your joy in giving, making other life's worth living. Today we say "thank you" for all that you do. You're wonderful vessels that God moves through, giving of yourselves for nothing at all obedient children who answered God's call. If it were not for people like you, we would be limited in what we could do. God bless you for all the joy that you bring for you give so much, expecting nothing.

The Road Of Life

While traveling down this road
Speed bumps will slow you down
Hills get high, valleys are low
Sometime we cry, leaving upon our face a frown.
This road of life is narrow
Not too many travel there
On this road are God's children
You won't find sinners anywhere
Satan is also on this road
Seeking whom he may devour
He'll throw curb balls of hatred, lies, deceit,
Backbiting and envy, but it doesn't stop there
We must be consistent to persevere
For its not easy, when satan is near.
Read God's Word and don't forget to pray. Give your
life to God, never fear.
Stay on this road of life
Put your hand in his hand
Jesus is walking right beside you
Leaving footprints in the sand.

We Have A Dream

We as black Americans have a dream. Our dreams and goals were buried deep within our spirits, deep within our minds and souls.

No one could even touch or destroy these dreams, thou many have tried. The spirituality and the reality of knowing God has kept our dreams alive.

So, I say to all of you, realize your dreams. Dr. Martin Luther King gave his life so that we could live our life to the fullest and connect to our dreams. His soul rest with God, but his spirit rest within our spirits.

We as black Americans were born to dream, achieve and become successful. Dr. Martin Luther King wrote and I quote "I have a dream".

We as senior citizens may not live to realize our dreams, but we can pass them on to our children and our grandchildren. Don't stop dreaming, never, never stop. Keep your dreams alive!

God Has Great Things In Store For You

As a man thinketh so is he, God has great things in store for you and me. He promises never to leave nor forsake. You can take him at His word—that's no mistake.

Never give up—always believe Him. God has great things in store for you and by faith you can receive them.

Never give up on God for He knows just what you need. In times of strife and sorrow, satan comes to destroy your seed.

Hold on tight and don't give in. God has great things in store for you. Fight the good fight of faith, pray, read His word daily and you shall win.

Stand on God's word—don't walk away. God has great things in store for you today. A sound mind, a pure heart, food to eat and the very air we breathe are all great things from God.

Praise and give Him thanks for all that he does. Sing unto Him a new song, God has great things in store for you.

A Servant Of God

Humble to praise each and everyday, a willing servant who would serve me without pay. Free—to be my humble servant.

Willing to give you time, willing to give advice, wiling to love your enemy is such a sacrifice.

Tearing down strongholds on front of the line, the battle you fight, standing on my word, you don't doubt that I'm right.

You are my free and humble servant, obedience is the key, up long nights, praying all day on your bended knees.

You are my free and humble servant, you have been set free. You witness to the captives and now they begin to believe.

You're my free and humble servant, a prophet I have called. You are willing to serve me even when your name is scolded.

So may God bless this day as you go on your way. And as I continue to give you words to say.

Bless you! My free and humble servant!

Busy As A Bee

Did you stop to say thank-you for breakfast and dinner or were you busy as a bee?

Did you ever appreciate the sunshine or the rain? Did you pretend not to see?

Did you listen to the birds singing and the sound of children playing or did you pretend not to hear?

Did you cuddle a newly born baby or feel the rose petals or do you pretend not to feel?

Did you stop and smell the roses or the fresh bread baking in the oven or did you pretend that you couldn't smell?

Never be too busy to enjoy the simple things in life. Look around and you'll see so many gifts that He has given you and me. Never be too busy to see God's beautiful creation. Don't be busy as a bee! Just look around.

Love

Love is the willingness to forgive. Forgiveness is letting go, looking for the good in others and sometime saying yes, when you want to say no.

Love is the willingness to share, always share with those in need and never forget to share a smile or a hug. Let others know you care.

Love means compromise and sacrifice, lending a helping hand, and always being nice. Love is the blood that Jesus shed for you and me, no greater sacrifice I know. Love causes us to shed many tears. You can't hide it, just let it show.

God's Love For Us Never Dies

Tears were rolling down my face as I prayed to God down on my knees. God said "get up, it's already done, man don't have the answer, I have the keys".

Don't give up and don't give in, God is just around the bend. Jesus loves me, His Word can't lie. He has a home for me on high.

Jesus stands at the door and knocks, draw nigh unto Him and wait for a sign, that still soft voice you'll find. Listen to this voice and obey. It'll never lead you astray.

When my heart aches, to Him I go. There's no other one who comforts and loves me so. He will not leave you comfortless. He sent the Holy Ghost.

Trouble comes and trouble goes. A cross we all must bear. Jesus proved His love for us when He died on the cross. Take your burdens to Jesus and leave them there.

It Hurts To Love

Sometime no matter what we do, the ones we love will be untrue. The more you give, the more they take. I'll just misuse you for my sake.

I'll do as I please, because I deserve the best. It hurts to love. Can you pass the test? To truly love is to forgive and forget, but isn't it funny how love turns to rejection, neglect, and hate.

It's easy to say "I love you" Lord. Are they just words or is it really true. It hurts to love. This I know for I've been hurt many times before. Thank you God, Your love doesn't make me blue.

My only son gave his life for you because He loved you so. However, you still choose to sin as I stand knocking on your door.

I won't break in because I'm a gentleman you see. Although it hurts to love, I'll just wait until you come to me.

The love I give is the greatest love of all. I promise never to leave you nor forsake you. My love doesn't hurt because my love is true.

Jesus Loves Me And You

Jesus loves me this I know, when my heart aches to Him I go. There's no other comforter greater than Him. With outstretched arm His love will show.

When life gets hard as it sometimes will, God will give you grace and mercy to climb that hill. He's walking right beside you each and every day. To lead the way there are angels all around. Keep your mind on Jesus and your feet planted firmly on the ground. Read His word daily—you'll surely get a crown.

Close your eyes and wait for a sign that still soft voice you'll find. Listen to this voice and do obey. He'll never lead you astray. His everlasting love for me means more than words can say. I've found it to be true, if you talk with Him, He'll talk to you.

I was praying to God, down on my knees. Tears were rolling down my face. He said get up, it's already done. Man don't have the answer, I have the keys.

Trouble comes and trouble goes. God's love for us will always show. Don't give up and don't give in. Your answer is just around the bend. Jesus loves me. His word can't lie. There's a home for us on high. What a glorious time it will be when Jesus' face we can see. It's all about His love for you and me.

Thank You For Loving Me

I love You more each day and I know You love me too. I don't have to guess, I dare let even one day go by without letting You know how grateful I am for so many blessings.

If I tried to remember all these blessings, I'd surely forget. Thank You for loving me, when I didn't even pay my debt. I fail the test.

Thank, You Lord for loving me, when I was in a world of sin. You could have pushed me aside, instead You kept giving me another chance.

You watched over and protected me for You could see deep within my heart to see clearly why I sinned.

Clinging to worldly things of life will not ease your heartaches and doing pains. Thank You for loving me when, I was doing my thing.

It's good to know that only God can give you peace within. Keep searching until you find Him, and you'll see that Jesus is the answer to all your needs and pains.

Loving Is Doing

Loving is doing the best you can for your family, neighbors and fellowman. Love is not jealousy and puffed up. It rejoices, when you're happy; it hangs with you, when the going gets tough.

Love does not listen to gossip and lies that others may bring, but instead seeks God for the truth and pray that what was heard just may not be the right thing.

Loving is sharing, whatever you have to give food, clothing, flowers, money or a kind word and a smile. It may be a greeting card, a kind word, compliment or just spending time with someone lonely.

Loving is doing, but it can be painful too. While your love for someone may be innocent and true, the person that you love may not love or understand you.

Doing for others brings joy to your heart, just try it and you'll see. Loving others brings joy and pain for the one you love don't always treat you the same. I thank God for Jesus, because His love for me will never change.

The Rock

There's a "rock" called Jesus Christ. This "rock" is neither large nor small. You can lean upon this "rock", it won't let you fall.

This "rock" is as pure as a piece gold. The many miracles Jesus wrought have never been told. You can carry this "rock" with you wherever you go, because—

This "rock" is Invisible.
This "rock" is Incredible.
This "rock' is Indescribable.
This "rock" is Invincible.
This "rock" is Jesus Christ
Jesus is the "rock of ages".
Jesus is the "reason for the season".
Jesus is your "redemption".
Jesus is __ __ __ "real in my soul".
Receive "Jesus Christ" as your "rock".

Food
for Thought

Food For Thought

Look up and live
Peace of mind comes from within, it cannot be bought or given.
If you're not happy today, take the time to make someone else happy.
Jesus is my best friend.
Put god first, others second, and yourself last.
If you have nothing to offer, give a smile.
Always give god your best.
Each new day is a gift from god.
Is your name in the book of life?
Confess your sins, ask for forgiveness; accept jesus as your lord and savior and you shall be saved.
Do unto others as you have them do unto you.
Do the right thing. Try to do your best.
Do give god praise, honor, and glory. Don't forget to pray.
Do read your bible each day. Instructions for living are there.
Do ask for forgiveness of your sins, for we all fall short.
Do remember those in need, the sick and shut-in, those in prison too.

Do look around outside to enjoy the simple things in life and the beautiness of this earth. It's such a great gift.
Do give and it shall be given unto you.
Do give of your time, a listening ear, a smile, a hug, and a helping hand.
Do love the lord with all your heart, mind, body and soul.
Jesus is the light, walk in it daily.
Let's keep christ alive in 2006.
Everybody ought to praise the lord.
Give god the highest praise hallelujah.
God is love.
Come where the presence of god dwells.
Come and go with me to our fathers house.
It's in my heart to serve the lord.
God is great give him glory.
Salvation is free.
Believe on the lord jesus christ and you shall be saved.
Beware of the company you keep.
Begin each day with thanksgiving in your heart.
Be th ankfull unto him and bless his holy name.
Be not deceived, god is not mocked, whatever you sow that shall you also reap.
Beneath his wings is love.
Be grateful.
B—is for bleeding heart.
The blood will never lose its power.
Jesus is lord and savior.

What the Word Says About Angels

Genesis 48:16. The Angel which redeemed me from all evil, bless the lads; and let my name be named on them, and the name of my fathers Abraham and Isaac; and let them grow into a multitude in the midst of the earth.

Psalm 34:7. The Angel of the Lord encampeth round about them that fear Him, and delivereth them.

Ecclesiastes 5:6. Suffer not thy mouth to cause thy flesh to sin; neither say thou before the Angel that it was an error: Wherefore should God be angry at thy voice, and destroy the work of thine hands?

Isaiah 63:9. In all their affliction He was afflicted, and the Angel of His presence saved them: in His love and in His pity He redeemed them; and He bare them, and carried them all the days of old.

Hosea 12:4. Yea, he had power over the Angel, and prevailed; he wept, and made supplication unto Him: He found him in Bethel and there he spake with us;

Matthew 13:39. The enemy that sowed them is the devil;

the harvest is the end of the world; and the reapers are the Angels.

Luke 22:43. And there appeared an Angel unto him from heaven, strengthening him.

John 5:4. For an Angel went down at a certain season into the pool, and troubled the water: whosoever then first after the troubling of the water stepped in was made whole of whatsoever disease he had.

I Corinthians 6:3. Know ye not that we shall judge Angels? How much more things that pertain to this life?

II Corinthians 11:14. And no marvel; for Satan himself is transformed into an Angel of light.

Hebrews 2:2. For if the word spoken by Angels was stedfast, and every transgression and disobedience received a just recompence of reward;

Hebrews 2:16. For verily he took not on him the nature of Angels; but he took on him the seed of Abraham.

Hebrews 13:2. Be not forgetful to entertain strangers; for thereby some have entertained Angels unawares.

I Peter 1:13. Unto whom it was revealed that not unto themselves, but unto us they did minister the things, which are now reported unto you by them that have preached the gospel unto you with the Holy Ghost sent down from heaven; which things the Angels desire to look into.

About The Author

The author was born and raised in Pelham, North Carolina to the wonderful parents of Mr. and Mrs. Howard Stanfield. This was a family of seven, of which, I am number four.

I was married and from this union came two lovely daughters and two marvelous grandsons.

I am a retired divorcee, who enjoys the simple things in life—reading, writing, painting, arts, and crafts.

I graduated from Caswell County High School in Yanceyville, North Carolina and attended Rockingham Community College, where I received a certificate in CNAI.

I received Jesus as my Lord and Savior at a very early age.

I was inspired to write poetry in 2003.

www.ingramcontent.com/pod-product-compliance
Ingram Content Group UK Ltd.
Pitfield, Milton Keynes, MK11 3LW, UK
UKHW041844190726
13854UKWH00002B/713

9 781425 109226